# GEOGRAPHY FACT FILES

# DESERTS

● ● ● ● ● ● ● ● ● ● ● ● ● ● ● ● ● ● ● ● ● ● ● ● ● ● ● ● ● ● ● ● ● ●

## Anna Claybourne

HODDER
*Wayland*

an imprint of Hodder Children's Books

# GEOGRAPHY FACT FILES

COASTLINES
DESERTS
MOUNTAINS
OCEANS
POLAR REGIONS
RIVERS

Produced by Monkey Puzzle Media Ltd

Gissing's Farm, Fressingfield, Suffolk IP21 5SH, UK

First published in 2004 by Hodder Wayland

An imprint of Hodder Children's Books

Text copyright © 2004 Hodder Wayland

Volume copyright © 2004 Hodder Wayland

| | |
|---|---|
| Editor | Nicola Edwards |
| Designer | Jamie Asher |
| Picture Researchers | Lynda Lines and Frances Bailey |
| Illustrator | Michael Posen |
| Consultant | Michael Allaby |

Printed in China

Cover: Badlands National Park, South Dakota, USA

Title page picture: Anti-desertification measures in Mauritania: villagers use bushes to keep sand dunes in place.

Brtitish Library Cataloguing in Publication Data

Claybourne, Anna

Deserts. – (Geography fact files)

1.Deserts – Juvenile literature 2.Desert ecology – Juvenile literature

I.Title

551.4'15

ISBN 07502 4395 3

## Acknowledgements

We are grateful to the following for permission to reproduce photographs: AKG-Images 17 bottom; Alamy 33 (Pintail Pictures), 36 (Christopher Cunningham); Corbis 3 bottom (Gallo Images), 5 bottom (Owen Franken), 15 bottom (Ed Kashi), 21 top (Gallo Images), 23 top (Kevin Schafer), 32 (Mark E Gibson), 34 (Raymond Gehman), 39 bottom (Craig Lovell), 41 (David Keaton), 42 (Peter Turnley); Ecoscene 7 bottom (Fritz Polking), 28 (Christine Osborne), 40 (Sally Morgan); FLPA 3 middle (Silvestris Fotoservice), 9 top (David Hosking), 9 bottom (Silvestris Fotoservice), 10 (Minden Pictures), 21 bottom (E and D Hosking), 23 bottom (Chris Mattison), 43 bottom (E T Davis), 44 (Wendy Dennis); Getty Images front cover; Hulton Archive 11 top; NASA 24 (Jacques Descloitres, Modis Rapid Response Team/GSFC); PA Photos 39 top (ABACA); Panos Pictures 1 (Clive Shirley), 12 bottom (Jean-Leo Dugast), 17 top (Chris Stowers), 19 bottom (Ray Wood), 19 top (Giacomo Pirozzi), 37 (Rhodri Jones), 38 (Mark Henley), 45 (Clive Shirley); Popperfoto.com/Reuters back cover right (Peter Andrews), 3 top (Kamal Kishore), 15 top (Kamal Kishore), 31 bottom (Kamal Kishore), 35 (Peter Andrews), 47 (Peter Andrews); Robert Harding Picture Library 14 (C Rennie); Science Photo Library 16 (Earth Satellite Corporation); Still Pictures 4 (D Escartin), 5 top (DRA), 13 top (Voltchev/UNEP), 25 (Stefan Mauris), 26 (Mark Edwards), 27 (W Ming/UNEP), 29 (Fred Bruemmer), 30 (Gerard and Margi Moss), 31 top (Adrian Arbib), 43 top (Mark Edwards).

Hodder Childen's Books

A division of Hodder Headline Limited

338 Euston Road, London NW1 3BH

# CONTENTS

The words that are explained in the glossary
are printed in **bold** the first time they are
mentioned in the text.

# WHAT IS A DESERT?

A desert is a place that's very dry – so dry that it can be hard for plants, animals and people to survive there. The word 'desert' means empty, deserted or abandoned. However, although deserts have fewer living things in them than other places, most are not actually empty. They have their own wildlife, farms, industries and even towns and cities.

## DEFINING A DESERT

Geographers (people who study the Earth) used to define a desert as a place that got very little rainfall – less than 250 mm per year. Today they are more likely to use a system called the **aridity** index (aridity means dryness). This compares the amount of rain a desert receives with the amount of water that evaporates from the ground or gets used up by animals and people. The results are shown as a number. For example, according to one aridity scale, a very dry desert area, such as the middle of the Sahara, could have a score of –90, while a less dry area, such as northern Nigeria which is on the edge of the Sahara, might have a score of –20.

## HOT AND SANDY?

In cartoons, deserts are always shown as boiling hot and covered in sand dunes. In fact, although many deserts are hot, some, such as the Gobi Desert in Mongolia and China, can be cold in winter. Even the hottest deserts, such as the Kalahari in southern Africa, can get very cold at night. Some of the coldest places in the world, including Antarctica, are also classed as deserts because they get very little rain. Also, only about a quarter of the world's desert is sandy. The rest is made up of bare rock or pebble-strewn plains.

**These sweeping sand dunes are in the Sahara Desert in Algeria. However, most deserts are more rocky than sandy.**

This satellite image shows part of Egypt, with the Sahara Desert on the left. The Gulf of Suez, part of the Red Sea, is at the top right.

## LIFE IN THE DESERT

The main problem for desert people and wildlife is how to find enough water. Many desert plants and animals are **adapted** (suited) to dry conditions, and don't need much to drink. Desert-dwelling people can get water from oases (see page 12), where water bubbles up from underground. They can also pump water out of the ground, or pipe it into the desert from somewhere less dry.

## LOCATION FILE

### THE SAHARA
The Sahara is the world's biggest desert. It stretches all the way across the northern part of Africa, overlapping 10 countries and covering 9 million km². About a fifth of it is sand dunes, and the rest is rocky. The name 'Sahara' is the Arabic word for desert.

**This photo shows a rocky part of the Sahara, with a Tuareg man leading his camel across the loose stones.**

# WHERE ARE DESERTS?

Although they can be very hot, deserts are mainly not found at the Equator, even though this is the part of the Earth that receives the most sunshine. Instead they occur north and south of the Equator, around the Tropic of Cancer and the Tropic of Capricorn. This is mostly because of the way massive air **currents** move around the Earth.

## HOT AIR

At the Equator, the air heats up and rises into the sky. As it rises, spreads out and cools, any water it is carrying falls as rain (making Equatorial regions very wet). The dried-out air then moves north and south to the **tropics**, where it finally sinks down to the ground and heats up. Because the air contains so little water, these areas rarely see any clouds or rain.

## DESERTS IN THE MIDDLE

Deserts are often found in the middle of large areas of land, because it's hard for rainclouds to get there (see page 8). There aren't many desert islands, because small islands usually get plenty of rain thanks to clouds that form from the sea around them.

### FACT FILE

**THE 10 BIGGEST DESERTS**
Apart from Antarctica, these are the world's biggest deserts:
• Sahara Desert, North Africa: 9,000,000 km²
• Arabian Desert, Middle East: 2,400,000 km²
• Gobi Desert, Central Asia: 1,300,000 km²
• Kalahari Desert, southern Africa: 950,000 km²
• Patagonian Desert, Argentina: 670,000 km²
• Great Victoria Desert, Australia: 650,000 km²
• Great Basin Desert, USA: 490,000 km²
• Chihuahuan Desert, Mexico: 450,000 km²
• Great Sandy Desert, Australia: 400,000 km²
• Kara Kum Desert, Turkmenistan: 350,000 km²

This diagram shows how air currents make some parts of the world very dry.

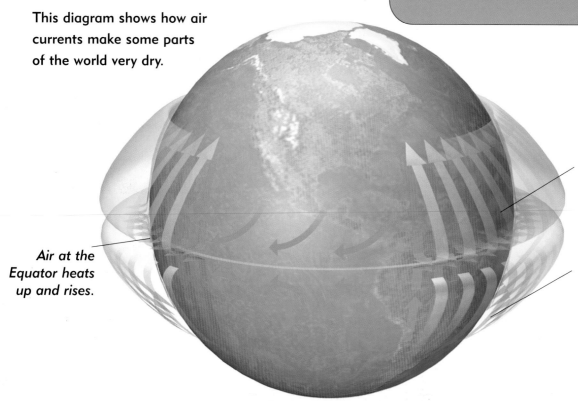

Air at the Equator heats up and rises.

The water in the air forms clouds and falls as rain.

The dry air is forced outwards to the tropics, where it sinks and gets hotter.

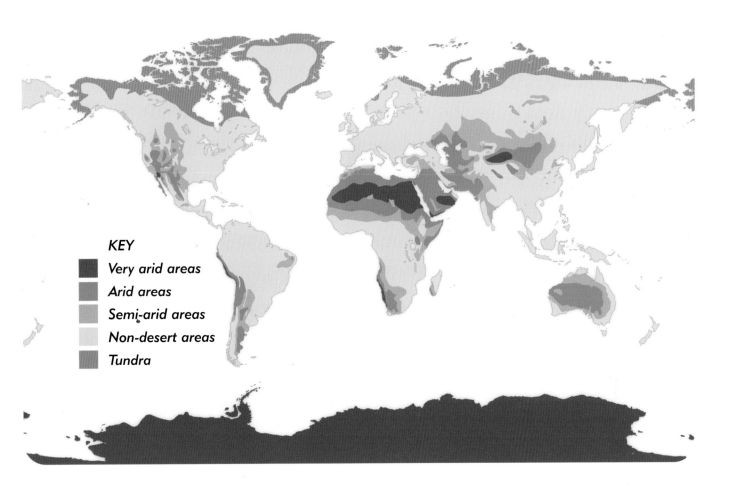

KEY

Very arid areas

Arid areas

Semi-arid areas

Non-desert areas

Tundra

This map shows the location of the world's main desert areas. Different colours show different amounts of rainfall and the darkest areas are the driest.

## ICY DESERTS

Icy areas such as Antarctica and the area around the North Pole are officially deserts. This is because, even though they are full of water, it's frozen solid, and there is very little rain. This makes it hard for plants and animals to get enough to drink, so, like a normal desert, these 'deserts' don't have as much wildlife as other places.

## LOCATION FILE

### ANTARCTICA

If Antarctica were a true desert, it would be the biggest in the world – at 14 million km², it's much bigger than the Sahara. Instead of rain, Antarctica gets mostly snow – but it's the equivalent of 50–200 mm of rain a year, well within the desert range. However, although Antarctica is a desert, it is very unlike most other deserts, and is often left out of desert books and lists. This is why the Sahara is usually called the world's biggest desert.

Left **Emperor penguins on the ice in Antarctica. Instead of having to find fresh water, emperor penguins drink sea water. They have a special gland that filters out the salt.**

# HOW DESERTS FORM

The main reason a desert forms is lack of rainfall. But why is there no rain? It's usually because rainclouds can't reach the area. Clouds lose their rain before they get there, leaving some parts of the world mostly cloud-free and very dry.

## WHERE CLOUDS COME FROM

Clouds form when air heats up and rises into the sky, then starts to cool. When this happens, the water vapour (water in the form of a gas) in the air **condenses** into droplets of water. As clouds rise, they get even colder, and this makes the water in them fall as rain.

Areas in the middle of large land masses, far away from the sea, can become deserts because clouds rarely travel far enough to reach them. As shown on page 6, areas around the tropics are also dry because clouds from the Equator fall as rain on their way there.

## RAINSHADOW DESERTS

A rainshadow desert happens when a range of high mountains stops rain from reaching a particular area. As damp air moves towards the mountains, it is forced to rise up. As it rises, it cools and forms clouds, and as they move higher up the mountains they drop their water as rain or snow. The air that then blows over the peaks is very dry. Clouds rarely reach the other side, and it hardly ever rains there. The Great Basin Desert in the USA is an example of a rainshadow desert.

### LOCATION FILE

#### DEATH VALLEY

Death Valley in California, USA is one of the world's hottest, driest places. Even though it's 85 m below sea level, it is incredibly dry, as it's in the rainshadow of the Sierra Nevada and Panamint mountains. It gets less than 50 mm of rain per year.

This diagram shows how a rainshadow desert forms.

*As it rises, the water vapour in the air condenses and forms clouds, which fall as rain.*

*Only dry air reaches the land beyond the mountains, making it a desert.*

*The air hits the mountains and is forced to rise.*

*Damp air blows in from the sea.*

## DESERTS BY THE SEA

Deserts sometimes form next to the sea, especially on western coasts. On some large land masses, air currents blow mainly from east to west. By the time they reach the west coast, the air has dropped most of its water as rain, and is very dry. So west-coast deserts receive very little rain, although they are sometimes covered in fog that comes off the sea.

## WHAT ARE DESERTS MADE OF?

Deserts are mainly made of bedrock – the rock that is left behind when soil dries out and is blown away by the wind. Sandy deserts are formed when weather makes rock gradually crack and crumble into particles. Sometimes, deserts are covered with minerals such as salt. This happens when rare rainwater dissolves minerals in the rocks. When the water **evaporates**, the minerals are left behind on the desert surface.

Some desert rocks even look as if they are painted, because minerals in them can react with the air to form coatings known as 'desert varnish'.

**The dunes of the Namib Desert on the coast of Namibia in Africa, where they meet the Atlantic Ocean.**

# HOW DESERTS CHANGE

Deserts change a lot. They can change slowly over time, as rock wears away and climates get warmer or cooler. And in sandy deserts, dunes are constantly moving, changing shape and rebuilding themselves.

## CHANGING CLIMATES

Over thousands of years, the Earth's climate changes, and deserts come and go. For example, dried-up waterways and plant fossils show that about 5,000 years ago, the Sahara was much greener and wetter than it is now. Scientists think it may have become a desert because of slight changes in the tilt of the Earth and its **orbit** around the Sun.

## AEOLIAN ACTION

'**Aeolian**' is a word geographers use to describe the action of the wind. It's named after Aeolus, the Greek god of the winds. In deserts, the wind is a powerful force. It 'transports' or moves particles of sand and dust around, changing the shape of the desert, or sometimes blowing them away completely so that only bare rock and boulders remain.

**Aeolian action has carved ridges into these desert rocks in Utah, USA. This happens when layers of soft rock are worn away faster than the layers of harder rock between them.**

## LOCATION FILE

### ULURU
Uluru, also known as Ayers Rock, is a massive rock dome in the middle of the Australian desert. It was formed over millions of years as **erosion** wore away the surrounding land, leaving the harder rock standing. The rock itself has been worn into a smooth rounded shape with ridged patterns.

## AMAZING SHAPES

In the desert, aeolian action can erode, or wear away, solid rocks. This happens because the wind picks up particles of sand or stone and carries them along. When they hit larger rocks, they gradually wear them away. This kind of erosion can cut patterns and textures in desert rocks, or carve them into strange shapes.

### R. A. BAGNOLD

R. A. (Ralph) Bagnold (right) was a British army officer who became one of the first people to study and understand sand dunes. Stationed in Cairo in the 1920s, he spent his spare time making field trips into the Sahara Desert to find out more about dunes. Today, dunes are studied using **satellites**, but Bagnold and his team drove into the desert in specially modified cars to measure the dunes.

**Ralph Bagnold (1896–1990) photographed in 1929, sitting on one of his specially modified desert cars.**

## DESERT DUNES

A dune is a naturally formed heap or ridge of sand shaped by the wind. Deserts with dunes include the Sahara, Arabian and Namib deserts. There are several different types of dunes. For example, barchan dunes are crescent-shaped, dome dunes are circular, and transverse dunes look a little like ocean waves.

## MOVING DUNES

Many types of dunes move slowly across the desert over time. Again, this happens because of the wind. It blows grains of sand away from one side of the dune and they collect on the other, gradually changing the dune's position. A barchan dune, for example, can travel across the desert at a speed of 20–30 m per year. As the sand in a sand dune moves, it can sometimes make a strange booming or singing sound.

**Barchan sand dunes viewed from above. The arrow shows the direction they move in.**

*Movement of sand grains*

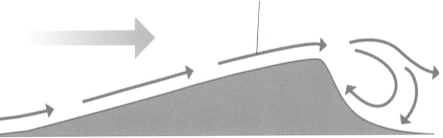

**Cross-section through a barchan sand dune. The dune moves forward as the wind blows grains of sand up its slope and over the top of it.**

11

# WATER IN THE DESERT

**D**eserts are dry, but they do have water in them. Often it's not on the surface, but stored in rocks underground. Sometimes this underground water comes to the surface and forms an oasis. Deserts can also have sudden showers of rain, flash floods and even a few rivers and lakes.

## WHAT IS AN OASIS?

An oasis is a freshwater spring that flows out of the ground in a desert. Oases can form where an aquifer – a layer of soil or rock underground that contains water – comes near to the surface. Aquifers can store water that has fallen as rain a long way away. As more and more water soaks into the rock, it can spread out underground and sometimes gets carried into desert areas.

*How an oasis forms.*

*Rain from other areas collects in underground rocks, creating an aquifer.*

*Where the aquifer touches the surface, water flows out, forming an oasis.*

## ⚙ LOCATION FILE

### THE DEAD SEA

The Dead Sea (right) is actually a salty desert lake in Israel and Jordan. It is formed by water from the Jordan River flowing into a low-lying desert area 412 m below sea level. The water continually evaporates in the desert heat, leaving behind the minerals and salts it contains. Today, the Dead Sea is 30 per cent salt. It gets its name because hardly anything, except for a few bacteria, can live in it.

**These lumps and crusts of salty minerals form along the edge of the Dead Sea as the water evaporates.**

This oasis in the Sahara Desert in Libya makes it possible for trees and farm animals to live in the desert.

## DESERT RAIN

Some deserts, though mostly dry, have rainy seasons. The Sonoran Desert in the USA, for example, has two rainy seasons: one in winter and one in summer. When the rain comes, desert flowers bloom for just a few weeks. Some very dry deserts can have sudden, unexpected rainstorms which cause flash floods. But as there are few plants and hardly any soil to soak the water up, it evaporates quickly, leaving the desert as dry as before.

## WADIS

A wadi, also known as an arroyo, is a desert river. Unlike most rivers, though, a wadi is usually empty, and fills up only on the rare occasions when it rains. Some wadis in the Arabian Desert and the Sahara are so big that geographers believe they were once proper rivers, at a time when these deserts were not as dry as they are today.

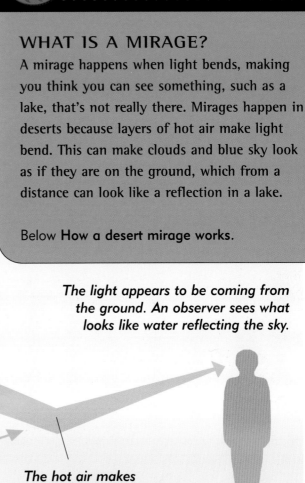

## FACT FILE

### WHAT IS A MIRAGE?

A mirage happens when light bends, making you think you can see something, such as a lake, that's not really there. Mirages happen in deserts because layers of hot air make light bend. This can make clouds and blue sky look as if they are on the ground, which from a distance can look like a reflection in a lake.

Below **How a desert mirage works.**

*Light from the sky*

*The light appears to be coming from the ground. An observer sees what looks like water reflecting the sky.*

*Layer of hot air above the ground*

*The hot air makes the light bend.*

# STUDYING DESERTS

Scientists go into deserts to study all sorts of things – plants and animals, rocks and minerals, fossils, weather, astronomy and ancient civilizations. There are still lots of things for them to find out.

## CLIMATE CHANGE

By measuring weather patterns and looking at landforms, fossils and other evidence, scientists can work out how a desert has changed, and whether it's becoming wetter or drier. For example, fossilized plant pollen, dried-up water channels and rock art left by ancient peoples reveal that the Sahara used to have more plants and animals in it in the past. Information like this provides useful clues about how the Earth's climate has changed as a whole, and how it might change in the future.

## THE NIGHT SKY

Large areas of desert have no towns, so they are very dark at night, and because there are so few clouds, the skies are very clear. This makes deserts great places to look at the stars from, and there are space **observatories** in deserts around the world.

## LOCATION FILE

### THE PYRAMIDS

Egypt's famous pyramids are in the eastern Sahara Desert. They contain the tombs of ancient Egyptians who lived around 5,000 years ago. The dry desert climate has helped to preserve the art, buildings and **mummies** (preserved bodies) at the site, providing us with huge amounts of information about the ancient Egyptians and how they lived. Archaeologists (people who study ancient remains) are still making new discoveries there.

These mummies were found in a 500-year-old cemetery in the desert near Nazca in Peru.

### DESERT DINOSAURS

Thousands of dinosaur skeletons have been found in deserts. Here are a few of them along with some of the places they have been discovered:

| DINOSAUR | WHAT WAS IT? | WHERE FOUND |
|---|---|---|
| Allosaurus | A fierce dinosaur that hunted in packs | Great Basin Desert, USA |
| Tyrannosaurus bataar | A large, recently discovered meat-eater | Gobi Desert, Mongolia |
| Paralititan | A huge plant-eater with a long neck and tail | Sahara Desert, Egypt |
| Argentinosaurus | Possibly the biggest dinosaur ever | Patagonian Desert, Argentina |

Above **A scientist clears dirt from a dinosaur vertebra (backbone) in the desert in Argentina, South America.**

## UNDER THE DESERT

One of the most important jobs for desert scientists is to find out what's underground in the desert. They look for oil and useful rocks and minerals which can then be extracted and sold. Or they look for water to supply local towns and cities. To find these things, scientists drill down into the ground to collect rock samples, or use advanced methods such as satellite technology (see page 16).

## STUDYING WILDLIFE

Many desert animals are rare and hard to find, so there are some species we still know very little about. Scientists sometimes have to spend weeks tracking desert creatures such as the Bactrian camel and the desert cat in order to study them.

**These Bedouin people are using a drill to find water under the ground in their desert home in Syria.**

# MAPPING DESERTS

**D**eserts were among the last places on Earth to be properly mapped. In the past, you could only make a map of somewhere by travelling across and measuring every part of it, and deserts are so remote and harsh that this was impossible. Even today, some desert areas have only been mapped by satellite.

## ON THE GROUND

To map an area from ground level, surveyors (scientists who measure land) find landmarks, such as rocks, hills or rivers. By measuring the distances and angles between landmarks, they can make an accurate scaled-down copy of them on paper – a map. They use a tool called a theodolite to line up landmarks and measure the angles between them. Modern theodolites fire a **laser** beam between landmarks to measure them as accurately as possible.

## HI-TECH MAPPING

Today, many desert maps are made not by surveyors on the ground, but by satellites orbiting the Earth. Satellites such as Landsat carry cameras which can take pictures of the Earth and beam them back down to the ground. Some satellites can also measure infra-red radiation, which tells them how hot or how dry the ground is, and some can measure the amount of vegetation, which tells them how dry the soil is. This makes them especially useful for mapping deserts. The information they collect is processed on computers and then made into maps.

## PEOPLE FILE

### AHMED MOHAMED HASSANEIN

Ahmed Mohamed Hassanein was an Egyptian politician and sportsman who, in the 1920s, became one of the first people to explore and map the Libyan Desert (part of the Sahara) scientifically. He made two expeditions, in 1921 and 1923, and returned with not only maps but also information about desert peoples and animals, desert geography and safe desert travel. He became a national hero in Egypt, where he was nicknamed the 'man of the desert'.

This is a satellite image of the city of Las Vegas in Nevada, USA, and the surrounding desert. Yellow and red areas show mineral deposits in the desert, while pale blue areas show where desert mining is taking place.

## MAPPING TOOLS AND TERMS

- **CARTOGRAPHY** A name for the science of creating maps. People who make maps are called cartographers.
- **GIS (Geographic Information Systems)** Computer technology that can process satellite or survey information and make it into maps.
- **GPS (Global Positioning System)** A system that analyzes information beamed from satellites to fix a position on the ground, using a handheld GPS receiver (right).
- **REMOTE SENSING** This is a name for finding out information about the Earth from a long way away – for example, by using a satellite.

**The man in the foreground is learning to use a GPS receiver to help make maps.**

## STILL UNEXPLORED

The Australian Outback is a huge arid area that takes up most of the interior of the continent of Australia. It includes several deserts. Experts think that some parts of these deserts have never been explored on foot because they are so hot, harsh and difficult to cross. It has only been possible to make maps of them using images from satellites, or by flying over them in planes.

**This map showing part of Africa dates from the sixteenth century. You can see the empty areas where the Arabian and Sahara deserts are.**

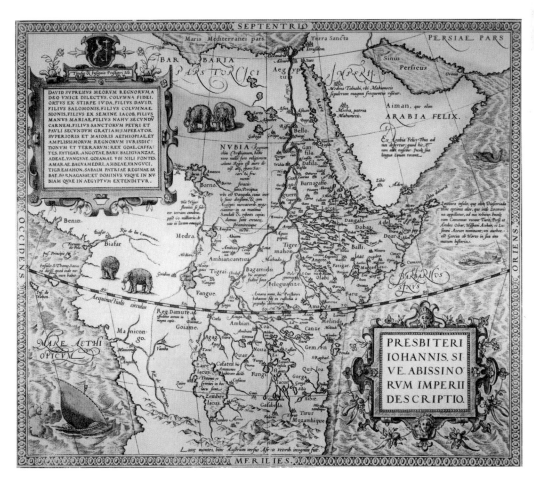

# DESERT ZONES

All deserts are dry, but some are drier than others. On maps of deserts, such as the one on page 7 of this book, you may see different colours used to show different degrees or zones of aridity (dryness). Around the edges of deserts, there are often **semi-arid** (or medium-dry) zones.

## FROM DRY TO VERY DRY

Usually, the driest part of a desert is in the middle. The zones radiate outwards in rings, with the less dry areas around the edge where the desert borders on other regions, such as forests or grasslands. Sometimes, the driest zones can be on western coasts (see page 9). Both these types of aridity patterns occur in Australia, for example.

## SEMI-ARID LANDS

A semi-arid area is not as dry as a true desert. In terms of rainfall, semi-arid lands receive between 250 mm and 1,000 mm of rain per year, although they usually have a dry season when there is no rain at all. They can support more plants and animals than a normal desert, and may be covered in sparse grass or bushes, or dotted with trees. Because the land can be used for farming, a lot of people live in semi-arid lands too – but they are constantly at risk of droughts and famines.

## THE SAHEL

The Sahel is one of the world's biggest and most famous semi-arid areas. It runs along the southern edge of the Sahara, overlapping countries such as Mali, Chad and Sudan, and is home to around 50 million people. Some parts of the Sahel go through long droughts with no rainfall, and famines there have caused millions of deaths.

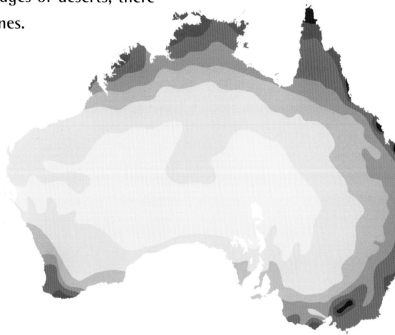

In this aridity map of Australia, the palest colours show the driest areas.

---

### FACT FILE

**DESERT DIVISIONS**

There are various ways of dividing arid lands up into different zones. Here is a common one:
- HYPER-ARID OR EXTREMELY ARID ZONE The driest deserts, with annual rainfall of less than 50 mm.
- ARID ZONE Deserts with up to 250 mm of rainfall.
- SEMI-ARID ZONE Medium-dry areas with 250–1,000 mm of annual rainfall.
- DRY SUBHUMID ZONE These slightly dry areas have between 1,000 mm and 2,000 mm of rain a year.

### SHRINKING LAKE CHAD

Lake Chad is a huge lake in the semi-arid Sahel region, south of the Sahara Desert. It provides water and fish for the people in the semi-arid parts of the countries that surround it: Niger, Chad, Nigeria and Cameroon. However, the lake is now shrinking thanks to droughts and human activities, such as using its water for **irrigation**. It is now just one-twentieth of the size it was in the 1960s.

**Children washing pots and pans in Lake Chad.**

### GETTING DRIER

Over time, a semi-arid land can dry out and become a complete desert. This can happen after a drought, when a semi-arid area goes without rain for so long that its plants die and its soil dries out into dust. Or it can happen if the land is over-used. This process is called **desertification**, and you can read more about it on page 42.

This picture shows Peul people outside their hut in Mali, in part of the Sahel.

# DESERT WILDLIFE

**T**o survive in the desert, plants and animals need special features or abilities that help them to resist extreme temperatures and find enough water. Over time, desert species have adapted, or become suited, to the dry desert **habitat** (surroundings).

## WATER SHORTAGE

Many desert plants and animals only need a small amount of water. Cacti, for example, have thick, waxy skin, and spines instead of leaves, so that not much water escapes from them into the air. Camels sweat very little, to avoid losing water from their bodies. Instead of drinking from streams or rivers, desert animals such as jerboas get the water they need from their food. Others, such as the thorny devil, a lizard from Australia, drink dew that collects on their bodies. Many desert plants have large root systems that spread out to catch as much rain as possible, or reach deep into the sand to suck up water from under the ground.

## FINDING FOOD

There is not much food in the desert, but as long as there's enough water for some plants to grow, animals can survive by feeding on them or eating other animals (see the food web on page 22). But many desert animals have to travel a long way to find their food. Camels, asses and other plant-eaters wander across the desert in search of plants to nibble. Meat-eaters such as coyotes and vultures constantly move around looking for prey or dead carcasses to feed on.

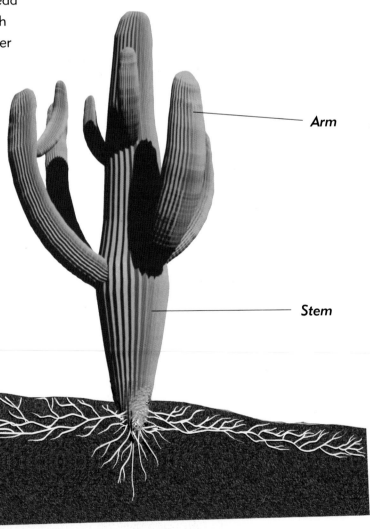

**A saguaro cactus. These huge cacti are found in deserts in North America and Mexico, and can grow up to 12 m tall.**

*Arm*

*Stem*

*Roots. Saguaros have shallow roots that spread out wide under the soil. When it rains, they soak up water very quickly before it has a chance to evaporate.*

## OUT AT NIGHT

Many deserts are so hot during the day that you could fry eggs on the ground, and there's very little shade. So a lot of desert animals, such as fennec foxes, bobcats, gerbils, and jerboas, are nocturnal (active mainly at night). They spend the day resting in a burrow or den. Because deserts are cold at night, a lot of nocturnal desert animals have thick, warm fur.

## AVOIDING THE HEAT

During the day, the sandfish (actually a type of lizard) avoids the hot sun by 'swimming' along just under the surface of the sand. Some other lizards lift their feet up in pairs to let them cool off. And some desert plants keep cool by being hairy – the hairs reflect heat away from their leaves and stems.

A shovel-snouted lizard from Africa lifting its feet up in pairs to keep them cool. This is known as a 'thermal dance'.

## FACT FILE

### SURVIVAL STRATEGIES

These desert-dwellers have special tricks for dealing with the desert:

• A camel can close not only its eyes, but also its nostrils to keep sand out.

• The banded gecko's eyelids have interlocking 'teeth' along the edges, so it can zip them closed against loose grains of sand.

• Fennec foxes (right) have huge ears. As well as being good for listening, they keep the fox cool by letting heat escape from its body.

• Lungfish survive when lakes dry out by burying themselves in the mud, sealed inside a cocoon, until the rain comes again.

A fennec fox resting close to its burrow. Fennec foxes live in the Sahara and Arabian deserts.

# DESERT ECOSYSTEMS

**A**n **ecosystem** is the name for a habitat, such as a desert, and the community of plants and animals that live in it. The living things in an ecosystem depend on each other for food. They also have to fit in with their surroundings in order to survive.

## FOOD CHAINS AND WEBS

A food chain is a sequence of living things, in which each creature is food for the next. For example, plants are eaten by locusts, locusts are eaten by snakes, and snakes are eaten by birds of prey. A food web is a system of interconnecting food chains that shows a whole ecosystem at work. Different deserts have different ecosystems, depending on how dry they are and where in the world they are found. The food web on this page shows part of an ecosystem in the Chihuahuan Desert in Mexico and the USA.

## LIVING WITH CHANGE

Many desert habitats change through the seasons, receiving rain just once or twice a year. Some desert animals have adapted to take advantage of these short wet seasons. The desert spadefoot toad, for example, is an **amphibian** and needs to breed in water. It lays its eggs in temporary pools that form in the rainy season, and the tadpoles hatch and grow in a few weeks, before the pools dry out again.

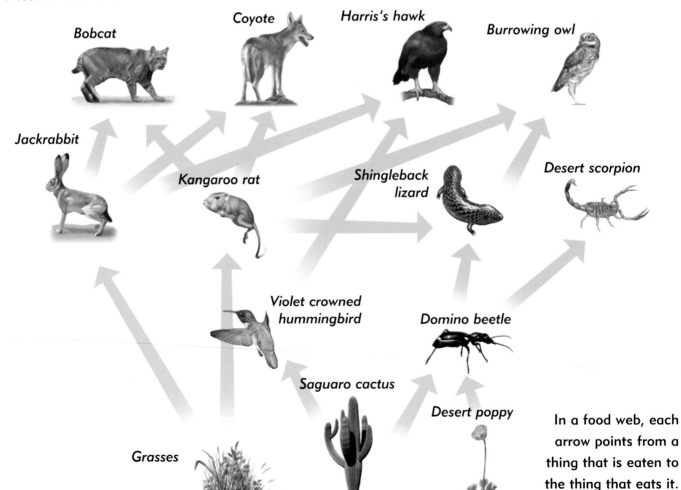

Bobcat

Coyote

Harris's hawk

Burrowing owl

Jackrabbit

Kangaroo rat

Shingleback lizard

Desert scorpion

Violet crowned hummingbird

Domino beetle

Saguaro cactus

Desert poppy

Grasses

In a food web, each arrow points from a thing that is eaten to the thing that eats it.

The desert spadefoot toad is usually only seen above ground after rain. It spends most of its time hiding in an underground burrow.

## SUMMER SLEEPING

Some desert animals, such as jerboas in the Sahara, spend the hottest, driest months asleep in an underground burrow. This is called **aestivating**. It's similar to hibernating, but it happens in the summer instead of in the winter.

## SPECIAL RELATIONSHIPS

Some plants and animals have relationships that help them both to survive. When living things work together in this way, it's called **symbiosis**. For example, the yucca plant, which lives in North American deserts, depends on the female yucca moth to carry its pollen to other yucca plants, so that it can make seeds. In return, the yucca gives the moth a place to lay its eggs, and provides food when they hatch out.

## FACT FILE

### DESERT CAMOUFLAGE

Most desert landscapes are made up of sand, pebbles or bare rock. Living things that want to camouflage themselves (blend in with their surroundings), in order to hide from predators or sneak up on their prey, often imitate the desert habitat.

• Pebble plants look just like pebbles.
• The desert horned lizard is flat and round, with speckled markings that look like sand.
• Desert scorpions can be a pale, sandy colour, or even almost transparent.
• A rattlesnake's brown and yellow markings make it hard for its prey to spot it against desert rocks – until it's too late!

**A speckled rattlesnake camouflaged against rocks in a Mexican desert.**

# DESERT WEATHER

**D**eserts can be incredibly hot, incredibly cold and incredibly windy. But why? One of the main reasons is the lack of plant cover. Without plants and trees to store moisture and stop wind, desert weather can easily reach extreme temperatures and conditions.

## HOT AND COLD

One reason deserts get so hot during the day and cold at night is that rock and sand heat up very quickly in the sun, and lose their heat quickly at night. In places with lots of soil, plants and water, this doesn't happen, as water and vegetation don't heat up and cool down so fast.

**A satellite image showing dust from the Sahara Desert being blown westward across the Atlantic Ocean.**

## FACT FILE

### DESERT WEATHER FACTS
• The world's hottest weather ever, a temperature of 58 °C, was measured in the Sahara Desert, at Al' Aziziyah in Libya, in 1922.
• If you count Antarctica as a desert, the world's coldest weather is in the desert too. The temperature in Vostok in Antarctica was measured at –89.2 °C on July 21, 1983.
• In 1968, showers of red dust fell on the UK. The dust had been blown from the Sahara, over 1,600 km away.
• Lightning in the desert can heat up sand so much, it turns into a type of glass called fulgurite.

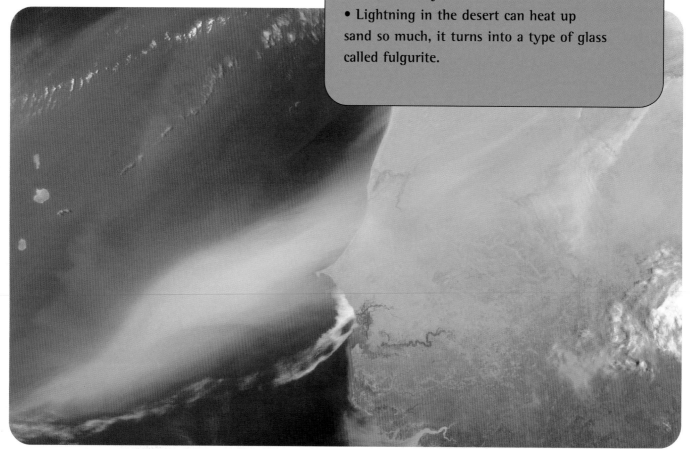

## WILD WINDS

In deserts, especially if they are very flat, wind can pick up speed over long distances, since there are few trees or houses in its way. In a sandy desert, strong winds can also pick up sand or dust and fling it into the air, causing sandstorms and dust storms. Sometimes, wind moves in a tight spiral, like a mini-tornado, and lifts sand or dust up in a tall, moving column. This is called a dust devil. According to Arabic legends, djinni, or genies, often took the form of a dust devil.

## RAIN AND SNOW

Some deserts have short rainy seasons, while others get a sudden, surprise rainstorm just once in a while. This usually happens because of an unusual weather pattern that blows clouds high over the desert, where it's cool enough for them to condense into raindrops. Even then, desert rain sometimes evaporates again before it hits the ground. If the air above the desert is very cold, the raindrops can sometimes turn into snow.

## LOCATION FILE

### THE SNOWY GOBI

The chilly Gobi Desert in Central Asia is one of the best places to see snow in the desert. In the summer, the Gobi can be warm, with temperatures of up to 40 °C, but in the winter it can be as cold as –30 °C. Snow combines with wind to cause blizzards, and sometimes covers the ground up to 15 cm deep.

**This snowy desert is in Monument Valley, Arizona, USA. In winter, the average temperature there is below freezing.**

# DANGERS AND DISASTERS

Deserts can be very dangerous. Both the extreme heat in the day, and the extreme cold at night can claim lives. People who travel in the desert have to take extra care not to get lost or run out of water. And people who live there also risk deadly dangers, such as drought, famine and sandstorms.

## DEADLY DROUGHTS

Many people live in desert or semi-arid areas such as the Sahel, where there is just enough water to survive. If the weather changes, and the rain they need doesn't arrive, it can cause a devastating drought. Besides causing a shortage of drinking water, droughts kill crops, so drought victims suffer from both hunger and thirst.

## LOST IN THE DESERT

It's easy to get lost in the desert because of the lack of roads and landmarks, and this has cost numerous desert travellers their lives. Without a source of water in a hot dry desert, a human being can only survive for a day or two. The daytime sun can cause terrible sunburn or deadly heatstroke. And when night falls and the temperature drops, it can be cold enough to cause **hypothermia**, which can also be fatal.

A farmer from Burkina Faso in the Sahel holding samples from his millet and sorghum crops. The crops on the right were grown in a good year. The much smaller, unhealthier ones on the left were grown in a year when there was a drought.

## FACT FILE

### DESERT SURVIVAL KIT
These items can save your life if you're lost in a desert:
• Blanket or coat for keeping warm at night.
• Umbrella to provide shade.
• Mirror for reflecting the sun and signalling to rescuers.
• Whistle for calling for help.
• Compass so you don't go round in circles.

A woman covers her eyes during a desert sandstorm in China.

## WHAT IS HEATSTROKE?

Heatstroke happens when a person's body heats up too much. The sufferer stops sweating, feels dizzy and confused, and may fall unconscious. Without medical help, they can fall into a coma – a long period of unconsciousness that's very hard to wake up from.

## SCARY SAND

Sandstorms can cause big problems for travellers and desert dwellers. The swirling sand makes it impossible to see, causing traffic accidents and even air crashes. In desert cities, such as Cairo in Egypt, people tape their doors and windows closed and stay at home until the danger is past. In the open desert, a big sandstorm can shift huge amounts of sand, sometimes completely burying vehicles or desert camps.

## PEOPLE FILE

### GILES AND GIBSON

Ernest Giles was a British-born explorer who tried to cross the deserts of Western Australia in the 1870s. On his second attempt, in 1873, he had to send his assistant, Alfred Gibson, to get help after one of their horses died. Gibson got lost in the desert, and was never seen again. Giles survived after a 100-km trek, during which he killed a wallaby with his bare hands and ate it raw. He later named the desert the Gibson Desert, after his missing companion.

# DESERT RESOURCES

Natural resources are the useful things we get from nature. Deserts contain many different kinds of natural resources, including sand, rocks and minerals, fuel, and useful plants and animals.

## DESERT MINERALS

Deserts are made of minerals, and many of them can be extracted and used in industry. Rocks such as granite and sandstone are used for building. Sand is an important ingredient of concrete, and is also used to make glass. Many deserts also contain other minerals such as phosphates, used to make fertilizers and detergents, and salt, which forms on the surface when water evaporates after soaking up salt from desert rocks. Precious minerals such as gold, agate and diamonds are also found in deserts.

**The buildings in the background of this picture, taken in the Sahara Desert in Sudan, are part of an oil refinery where crude oil is processed.**

## DESERT OIL

The most important desert resource of all is **crude oil** (which means oil that hasn't yet been refined and processed). It's found in many deserts, stored deep down in underground rocks. Crude oil is used to make fuel for things like power stations, cars and planes, and it provides the world with a lot of its energy – so it's in great demand, and very valuable. Some of the world's biggest oil fields are in deserts in places like the Middle East, northern Africa and the south-western USA. The oil was formed millions of years ago, when these areas were swamps or even seas. Over time, dead plants and animals were compacted (squashed) down by layers of rock and sand and eventually turned into oil.

## FACT FILE

### ARABIAN OIL

• About a quarter of the world's oil comes from the Arabian Desert in the Middle East.
• Arabian oil was first discovered in the 1930s. Today, Saudi Arabia is the world's biggest oil producer, with Iran, Iraq, Kuwait and the United Arab Emirates not far behind.
• The world uses up about 80 million barrels of oil per day. (One barrel holds 190 litres or 42 gallons.)

## DESERT ENERGY

As well as being full of oil, deserts provide us with energy in other ways. They're a very good place to put solar power plants, which collect energy from the sun, as the skies are clear and there's plenty of hot sunshine. Wind farms are often put out in the desert too, as the winds are strong and there's plenty of space for the wind turbines.

## PLANTS AND ANIMALS

People have been making use of desert plants and animals for centuries. The aloe vera plant from Africa is one example – the ancient Greeks and Sumerians used it as a medicine and beauty treatment, and it's now grown around the world and used in body lotion, shampoo and washing powder. Desert people **domesticated** wild desert animals such as the camel and the ass, because they were naturally tough and could survive harsh conditions. And some desert animals, like the bobcat and Arabian oryx, have been hunted for their horns, skin or fur.

An aerial view of a solar power station in the desert in California, USA. It collects the energy from sunlight and converts it into electricity for homes and factories. You can see the sun reflecting off the solar panels at the top of the picture.

 **LOCATION FILE**

### SOLAR TWO

Solar Two was a temporary experimental solar power plant built in the Mojave Desert in California, USA in 1995. It was set up to test how effective the new solar power technology might be. The power plant collected heat from the sun and stored it in molten salt. While it was operating, Solar Two could provide enough power for 10,000 homes. There are now plans to use the technology in bigger solar power plants to provide more energy.

# DESERT PEOPLE

Although deserts are harsh and inhospitable, with extreme temperatures and serious water shortages, humans have lived in them for thousands and thousands of years. Today, more people than ever are moving into the desert, as we run out of space for our cities and towns.

## DESERT NOMADS

In the past, the shortage of food and water in the desert meant that many desert people had to keep moving themselves and their animals around in order to find enough to eat and drink. This is called a nomadic lifestyle. Nomadic peoples include the Tuareg of the Sahara, and the Bedouin of the Arabian Desert. Today, though, these people are just as likely to live in permanent settlements with a piped-in water supply, such as Rahat in Israel.

## THE SAN OF THE KALAHARI

The San live in and around the Kalahari Desert in southern Africa. Many San now live in towns, but a few still have a traditional 'hunter-gatherer' lifestyle, hunting animals such as antelopes, and gathering berries, nuts, roots and eggs. This lifestyle is thousands of years old, and experts think that in the past, all humans lived this way.

## LOCATION FILE

### THE NAZCA LINES

Part of the Peruvian Desert in Peru is covered in hundreds of lines, geometric shapes and huge drawings of animals. They were created by the Nazca people, who lived in this area around 2,000 years ago. Experts disagree about what the lines were for, but some think they may have been used for religious rituals.

**This huge image of a spider is one of the desert drawings at Nazca. It is 45 m long.**

Nomadic people in Mongolia watching TV outside their traditional yurt.

## DESERT HOMES

Desert nomads need homes that can be moved easily. In the Sahara, Arabian and Gobi deserts, traditional nomads live in tents made of leather, wool or camel hair, which can keep the heat out during the day, and the cold out at night. More permanent desert houses are often built of mud, stone or concrete, and painted white to reflect heat away.

## DESERT CLOTHING

You might think hot weather means wearing fewer clothes, but in the desert, that's not a good idea. Burning rays of sun and gritty sand carried on the wind mean it's better to cover up. A traditional Tuareg man's outfit, for example, includes a long, loose cotton shirt and robes, and a veil worn over the face to keep sand out. Many desert people wear white clothes, as white reflects heat and so helps you to keep cool.

 **LOCATION FILE**

### THE THAR DESERT

The Thar Desert, which covers parts of Pakistan and northern India, is home to over 12 million people, making it one of the world's most heavily populated deserts. People there work in desert mines, or raise animals and crops using water carried into the desert in canals.

These women live in part of the Thar Desert near Jaisalmer in India. They are walking to work wearing pale clothes and veils to protect their faces, and carrying their work tools on their heads.

# DESERT TOWNS

Countries that are mainly desert, such as Libya, Algeria and Australia, tend to have most of their towns and cities along the coast. But there are settlements in the middle of deserts too. They range from tiny, temporary tent villages to huge cities like Phoenix in the United States and Riyadh in Saudi Arabia.

## TEMPORARY TOWNS

Nomadic desert people, such as traditional Bedouin herders in Jordan and Syria, may stay in one place for just a few weeks or months at a time. While they're there, they set up a temporary settlement. They put up their tents near a water supply and take their goats, sheep and camels to graze nearby. When water supplies or food for the animals run out, they take down their tents and move somewhere else.

## AROUND THE OASIS

Where an oasis provides a water supply, or there is a well or a pipeline to supply water, it's possible to build more permanent towns and villages. There, as long as there is enough water to irrigate the lands, people can set up farms with fields for crops and pens for animals.

**Las Vegas, a city in the Mojave Desert in Nevada, USA.**

## DESERT CITIES

Here are some of the world's most famous desert towns and cities:

| CITY | WHERE IS IT? | POPULATION |
|---|---|---|
| Alice Springs | Simpson Desert, Australia | 30,000 |
| Cairo | Sahara Desert, Egypt | 10 million |
| Las Vegas | Mojave Desert, Nevada, USA | 0.5 million |
| Phoenix | Sonoran Desert, Arizona, USA | 1.3 million |
| Riyadh | Arabian Desert, Saudi Arabia | 4 million |

## DESERT CITIES

It is possible to build a big city in the desert, as long as enough water and food can be transported into it to support the people who live there. For this reason, big desert cities are usually found in wealthy countries such as Saudi Arabia and the USA, which can afford to build major roads and pipelines, dams or underground pumping systems to supply water. Cities need a huge amount of water – for example, a city with a million people needs more than 200 billion (200,000,000,000) litres of water a year. Some cities, such as Phoenix in the USA, use so much water that the rivers and aquifers they take it from are in danger of running dry.

# LOCATION FILE

## KUWAIT CITY

Kuwait City (right), the capital of Kuwait, is on the coast of the Persian Gulf. There aren't enough fresh water sources nearby for its population, so the Kuwaitis take water from the sea, process it to remove the salt, and store it in huge water towers.

**These beautiful water towers, opened in 1979, are one of Kuwait's most famous landmarks.**

# DESERT FARMS

**M**any desert farmers don't have farms – they just move their herds of animals from place to place, finding water wherever they can. To grow crops in the desert, farmers usually have to use irrigation, or keep their crops near a water supply such as an oasis.

## DESERT FARM ANIMALS

Desert farm animals, such as camels, barbary sheep (also called aoudads), and Nubian goats, have been bred from wild animals that are at home in the desert. This means they are naturally suited to dry, difficult conditions and can survive without much water. Donkeys, known for their toughness, were also domesticated from desert species, such as the Somali ass.

**Circular areas of irrigated farmland in the desert in Nevada, USA. They have been watered by a rotating irrigation system which moves in a circle.**

## IRRIGATION

Irrigation means supplying land with water using pipelines, canals, ditches or other artificial methods. It can turn dry land, even a desert, into fertile land that can be used for growing crops. Many previously desert areas around the world have been turned into farmland.

## DESERT CROPS

The crops that grow best in the desert are those that naturally prefer dry conditions. They include corn, grown in Mexico and the USA, millet and sorghum in Africa and the Middle East, and citrus fruits, olives and date palms, often seen in Saharan countries such as Algeria and Morocco.

## THE INCREDIBLY USEFUL CAMEL

The camel (below) is probably the most useful desert animal of all. Over 90 per cent of the world's camels are now domesticated, and dromedary camels (which have one hump) no longer exist in the wild at all. Domestic camels are mainly kept by farmers and herders in African and Asian deserts.

Camels hardly ever sweat or pant, and this helps them to avoid losing water. A camel can go without a drink for several days.
A camel can cover 40 km in a day, even in the hottest desert conditions. Camels also provide meat, milk and leather.

Below **A domesticated dromedary camel.**

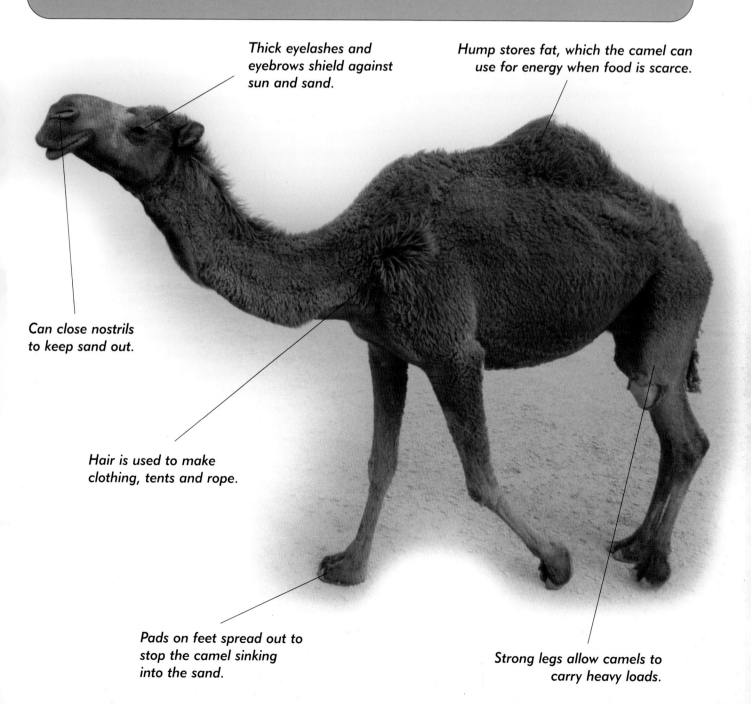

*Thick eyelashes and eyebrows shield against sun and sand.*

*Hump stores fat, which the camel can use for energy when food is scarce.*

*Can close nostrils to keep sand out.*

*Hair is used to make clothing, tents and rope.*

*Pads on feet spread out to stop the camel sinking into the sand.*

*Strong legs allow camels to carry heavy loads.*

# DESERT INDUSTRIES

The biggest industrial operations in deserts are oil extraction and mining. People also make money from setting up casinos and other attractions to entertain tourists (see page 38). And deserts are home to many cottage industries, where people make a living from traditional small-scale art, crafts and manufacturing.

## DRILLING FOR OIL

Most crude oil in deserts is trapped thousands of metres underground. To get it out, oil workers bore a deep hole in the ground, using a long drill shaft supported by a structure called a derrick. The oil may bubble up out of the ground itself, or it may have to be pumped out. Then it's usually carried away, by road, by sea or in a pipeline, to a refinery to be converted into useful fuel products.

**An oil-drilling derrick in the desert in Texas, USA, where there are lots of oilfields.**

## FACT FILE

### OIL: SUPPLY AND DEMAND
• We have already used up about half of the Earth's oil reserves.
• Many experts claim world supplies of oil will be used up by around the year 2050.
• At the moment, world demand for oil is rising, as more and more people drive cars and buy high-energy appliances. But as oil becomes more scarce, it will become more expensive, making it harder for people to afford gasoline and power.
• As oil gets used up, we will need to find other energy sources. Deserts could be useful for this, as they can provide plentiful solar and wind power.

## LOCATION FILE

### NAMIBIA'S DIAMOND MINES

In the coastal Namib Desert in Namibia, southern Africa, diamonds are buried in the loose gravel under the sand dunes. Lots of people have had to be rescued after going into the desert to find the diamonds, then getting lost or running out of water. Because of this, the whole area is now closed to the public. A single diamond mining company mines the diamonds by digging up the gravel and sifting through it.

## SMALL-SCALE INDUSTRIES

As well as farming, many desert people process and sell desert products to make a living. Traditional or cottage industries include collecting salt from the desert surface, which is still done in parts of the Sahara, and making rugs, blankets and clothes from the hair or wool of camels and desert sheep and goats. Native Americans from desert areas in Mexico and the USA make traditional silver and jade jewellery to export or sell to tourists. In Australia, aboriginal peoples make and sell traditional art, carvings and craft items such as didgeridoos.

**This man is selling salt, collected in the Sahara Desert, at a market in Mali.**

# DESERT TOURISM

Why would anyone go on holiday to the desert? Many people, especially those who live in big cities, like to escape from modern life to visit wild, unpopulated places where they can see beautiful landscapes and wildlife. Today, with new desert activities, sports and events being set up, there's more than ever to see and do in the desert.

## DESERT ACTIVITIES AND SPORTS

Popular desert activities include desert trekking and camping, and desert touring in 4-wheel-drive vehicles or on camels. For even more adventurous tourists, there's dune rally driving – driving specially modified cars over sand dunes – and sand skiing. Desert tours and activities can be expensive, but in oil-rich countries such as Saudi Arabia, the United Arab Emirates and the USA, there are plenty of people who want to pay for them, as well as visitors from other countries. Their money helps to provide income for desert people.

## JOBS IN TOURISM

Many people who live in deserts make a living from desert tourism. In the Sahara, for example, some Tuareg and Bedouin people work as desert guides, using their local knowledge to lead groups of visitors safely through the desert. In desert cities such as Jaisalmer, India and Las Vegas, USA, hotels, restaurants and casinos provide thousands of jobs for local people.

**Tourists admiring the Sphinx, an ancient sandstone carving at Giza in the Sahara Desert in Egypt.**

## FROM PARIS TO DAKAR

The Paris-Dakar Rally takes place in January every year. Competitors drive specially modified desert rally cars from Paris to Morocco and across the Sahara Desert, through Mauritania and Mali, to Dakar, the capital of Senegal. As well as those taking part, the rally brings support crews, spectators and journalists to these desert countries, boosting their tourist industries.

**A desert rally car driving over a sand dune in the 2003 Paris-Dakar Rally.**

## AMAZING SIGHTS

As they are often wild and undeveloped, deserts are a great place for tourists to spot wildlife such as birds, snakes and lizards, or to get a good look at the stars at night. People visit deserts to see stunning scenery too, such as the Grand Canyon in Arizona, USA, and Uluru (also called Ayers Rock) in the Australian Outback. The dry air in deserts also helps to preserve ancient ruins, such as the pyramids and the Sphinx in Egypt, and the ancient city of Teotihuacan in Mexico, which are major tourist attractions.

# LOCATION FILE

## JAISALMER

Jaisalmer in India is on the borders of the Thar Desert, and has developed a desert tourist industry. Tourists can go on camel rides, visit a desert national park to see wildlife, or look at dinosaur fossils from the desert in the Desert Museum. In the winter, Jaisalmer holds a desert festival, with camel races and traditional dancing and music.

**A camel race taking place during a camel fair in Pushkar, near Jaisalmer.**

# MANAGING DESERTS

Tourism, industry, irrigation and farming bring money to desert areas and help people survive, but they can also cause pollution, erosion and damage to ecosystems. Managing deserts means keeping control of the way deserts are used, so they don't get damaged and natural resources are not all used up.

Barbed wire and other litter left in the Sahara Desert in Egypt, near the pyramids. It may have been left there by builders or farmers.

## CHANGING THE DESERT

Many of the ways we use deserts change them so that they are no longer really deserts. For example, irrigating a desert makes it into farmland, and building mines, oil derricks, big roads and refineries in a desert reduces the area of undisturbed natural habitat.

Governments of desert countries can manage these changes by limiting the amount of land desert farmers and companies are allowed to use, so that some desert areas can be left alone and unchanged.

 **LOCATION FILE**

### DESERT IN MINIATURE

Alice Springs Desert Park, in Australia, is a managed wildlife park containing a selection of desert wildlife from the surrounding area. Visitors can explore desert habitats and ecosystems without having to go out into the rest of the desert, where they might get lost, leave litter or disturb endangered species.

## USING UP WATER

Pumping water into the desert to supply desert cities and farms uses up a lot of water. Water pumping schemes work best if they are 'sustainable', which means they can keep going without running out. Unfortunately, many desert irrigation and water supply systems today are not sustainable. For example, farming in the Sahel, and large cities in US deserts, are using up rivers, lakes and underground water reserves which will soon run out.

## MANAGING TOURISM

Tourists come to wild areas like deserts to appreciate the beauty of nature – but they also bring problems with them. Hotels, airports, roads and shops displace (move aside) wildlife and local people, and the tourists' litter and sewage has to be disposed of. So to keep deserts wild, governments have to keep control of tourism and leisure developments. They may make laws to protect wildlife, restrict building work and keep visitors out of some areas. In the USA, for example, there are laws to stop people from driving certain types of large vehicles such as SUVs or 4x4s in some desert areas, because of the damage they can cause to desert scenery, plants and animals.

## LOCATION FILE

### JOSHUA TREE NATIONAL PARK

A national park is an area of land that's set aside and protected from overdevelopment. Joshua Tree National Park in California, USA is an example of a desert national park. It has tourist facilities such as information centres, litter bins and toilets, and visitors pay an entrance fee. In return, an area of natural desert and its wildlife are kept safe for everyone to enjoy.

A tent in Joshua Tree National Park, next to a Joshua tree, the desert tree that gives the park its name.

# DESERTS IN DANGER

Deserts have been changing naturally for millions of years. But today, human activities such as water pumping, farming, mining, hunting and war are changing desert environments faster than ever. This can damage their delicate ecosystems and threaten their wildlife and people.

## DRYING OUT

Because deserts are so dry, the little water they do have is very important. Occasional rains, floods and oases allow a limited number of desert plants, animals and people to survive in a delicate balance. But now, irrigation, tourism and desert cities are in danger of using up underground water supplies and making some desert habitats too dry for anything or anyone to survive.

## ARE THE DESERTS GROWING?

Over the past 50 years, some experts have claimed that some deserts, especially the Sahara, have got bigger as the semi-arid land surrounding them has dried out. They have called this process 'desertification'. However, other experts disagree, saying the deserts may in fact be shrinking.

If desertification is happening, it could be caused by natural climate change, by people and crops using up too much water, or by herd animals eating too many plants, so that they no longer hold the soil together and it blows away in the wind. Scientists are still studying deserts to find out if desertification is happening and how it works.

## ☀ LOCATION FILE

### GULF WAR BATTLEFIELDS

Many wars have been fought in Middle Eastern desert lands such as Iran, Iraq and Kuwait. Soldiers and tanks crash through desert vegetation and leave litter and waste, and oil wells are sometimes set alight as an act of war. This causes massive pollution which can destroy the habitats of desert wildlife.

Burning oil wells fill the desert in Kuwait with polluting smoke at the end of the 1991 Gulf War.

Goats, sheep and cattle grazing on sparse vegetation in Burkina Faso in the Sahel, Africa.

## WILDLIFE IN DANGER

Besides running out of water, desert plant and animal species can be endangered by pollution, hunting, and loss of their natural habitats when desert areas are turned into roads, farms or cities. For example, the Gila monster, a large, venomous lizard from the deserts of Central America and the USA, is threatened for several reasons. Its natural habitat is shrinking as people build farms, roads and towns; it has been hunted and killed by people who are afraid of its poison; and young Gila monsters are often collected from the wild to be sold as pets.

 FACT FILE

### ENDANGERED DESERT ANIMALS

These desert species are in danger of dying out and becoming **extinct**:
• ARABIAN ORYX This long-horned antelope is hunted for its horns, skin and meat.
• DESERT TORTOISE America's rare desert tortoise is threatened by habitat loss and disease.
• BACTRIAN CAMEL This wild two-humped camel from the Gobi Desert is at risk from habitat loss, hunting and competition with farm animals for food.
• ADDAX Hunting and food shortages are threatening the addax, a Saharan antelope.
• INDIAN DESERT CAT This and other desert cats are endangered by hunting, road traffic and diseases caught from domestic cats.

**The Gila monster, once common in the deserts of the south-western USA, is now rare and threatened with extinction.**

# CONSERVING DESERTS

The millions of people living in desert areas need water and food, and must take them from their surroundings to survive. Many of them cannot afford to think about keeping the deserts as they are and saving desert species. However, there are some things governments and individuals can do to conserve, or save, desert areas for the future.

## TAKING CONTROL

One of the best ways to conserve deserts is to stop over-using land, water and other desert resources. That's easier said than done, but some progress is being made. Desert cities use laws and payment systems to limit people's use of water and stop them from wasting it. Farmers can save water by using irrigation methods such as drip irrigation, which waters the soil from below ground so that less water escapes into the air.

## LOCATION FILE

### CONSERVING THE KALAHARI

The Kgalagadi Transfrontier Park is a nature reserve in South Africa and Botswana. It conserves part of the Kalahari Desert and its wildlife, and protects them from overdevelopment. The reserve also keeps an area of land safe so that San people who wish to maintain their traditional hunter-gatherer lifestyle can do so in peace.

This picture shows a group of meerkats, one of the many different kinds of wildlife that live in the Kgalagadi Transfrontier Park.

### WHAT YOU CAN DO

If you go trekking in the desert, or visit a desert national park, you can help to protect the desert and its wildlife by following these guidelines:

• Don't start campfires! Dry desert grasses and shrubs easily catch fire.

• Take any litter away with you or put it in a bin.

• Keep to paths to avoid getting lost or disturbing wildlife.

• Never take plants, eggs or other natural objects away from a desert.

• At home, try to save energy to reduce pollution and climate change.

• If you live in a desert city such as Phoenix, Arizona in the USA, avoid wasting water.

### HELPING WILDLIFE

To protect desert plants and animals, governments set aside national parks and wildlife reserves where it's illegal to build anything or damage wildlife. Some reserves are devoted to protecting a particular species, such as the desert tortoise or the addax. Governments can also pass laws to make hunting and killing endangered desert animals illegal. In some areas, people can hunt desert animals, such as the bobcat, only with a permit and at certain times of year, to give the animals a chance to survive and recover their numbers. In many deserts, it's also illegal to collect wild flowers or other plants.

**These people in Mauritania, are using bushes to hold sand dunes in place, so that the desert doesn't spread right across their village.**

# GLOSSARY

**Adapt** When a plant or animal species adapts, it changes over time to suit its habitat.

**Aeolian** To do with wind.

**Aestivating** Spending the summer, or the hottest part of the year, in a kind of deep sleep.

**Amphibian** A type of animal, such as a frog or a toad, that can live on land but lays its eggs in water.

**Arid** Another word for dry.

**Condense** To change from a gas, such as water vapour, into a liquid.

**Crude oil** Oil in its raw state, before it is refined and processed.

**Current** A stream of moving water or air.

**Desertification** The process of becoming a desert.

**Domesticate** To breed and tame wild animals in order to use them as working or farm animals.

**Ecosystem** A habitat and all the plants and animals that live in it.

**Erosion** Wearing away of rock and soil.

**Evaporate** To change from a liquid, such as water, into a gas, such as water vapour.

**Extinct** If a plant or animal species is extinct, it has died out forever.

**GIS (Geographic Information System)** Computer technology used for making and displaying maps.

**GPS (Global Positioning System)** Technology that works out the positions of points on the globe using satellites.

**Habitat** The place where a plant or animal species lives, such as a desert or a forest.

**Hypothermia** A serious illness caused by the body becoming too cold.

**Irrigation** Channelling or piping a supply of water to an area of land to water it and make it fertile.

**Laser** (short for Light Amplification by Stimulated Emission of Radiation) A machine that sends out a concentrated beam of light.

**Mummy** A dead body that has been preserved over a long time.

**Observatory** A building designed for looking at something, such as the night sky.

**Orbit** The path of one object as it moves, or orbits, around another object.

**Remote sensing** Recording information about the Earth from far away, usually by using satellites.

**Satellite** A machine sent up into space to orbit the Earth. Some satellites are used to take photos of the Earth or record other geographical information.

**Semi-arid** A geographical description that means dry, or arid, but not as dry as a true desert.

**Subhumid** A geographical description that means slightly dry, or not humid (humid means damp).

**Symbiosis** When two plant or animal species live together in a way that helps both partners.

**Tropics** Two imaginary lines around the Earth, around 2,400 km north and south of the Equator.

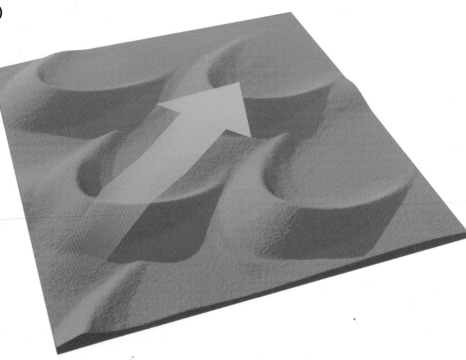

# FURTHER INFORMATION

## WEBSITES TO VISIT

**http://mbgnet.mobot.org/sets/desert/index.htm**

A site belonging to the Missouri Botanical Garden, with facts about deserts and their wildlife.

Missouri Botanical Garden
P.O. Box 299, St Louis
Missouri 63166-0299
USA
Tel: 314-577-5100

**http://www.enchantedlearning.com/biomes/desert/desert.shtml**

An Enchanted Learning site about desert habitats, including information on deserts of the world and desert animals, with lots of pictures.

Enchanted Learning
P.O. Box 321, Mercer Island
WA 98040-0321
USA
Email: other@EnchantedLearning.com

**www.alicespringsdesertpark.com.au/default.htm**

Take a virtual tour of the Alice Springs Desert Park in Australia.

Alice Springs Desert Park
Larapinta Drive, P.O. Box 1046
Alice Springs NT 0871
Australia
Tel: +61 8 8951 8788
Email: asdp@nt.gov.au

## BOOKS TO READ

**Horrible Geography: *Desperate Deserts*** by Anita Ganeri (Scholastic Children's Books, 2000)

**Mapping Earthforms: *Deserts*** by Catherine Chambers (Heinemann Library, 2001)

**Biomes Atlases: *Deserts and Semideserts*** by Michael Allaby (Raintree, 2004)

**Eyewitness: *Desert*** by Miranda MacQuitty (Dorling Kindersley, 2000)

# INDEX